HowE

How To Jiu Jitsu For Beginners

Your Step By Step Guide To Jiu Jitsu For Beginners

HowExpert with Nathan DeMetz

Copyright HowExpert™
www.HowExpert.com

For more tips related to this topic, visit HowExpert.com/jiujitsu.

Recommended Resources

- HowExpert.com – Quick 'How To' Guides on All Topics from A to Z by Everyday Experts.
- HowExpert.com/free – Free HowExpert Email Newsletter.
- HowExpert.com/books – HowExpert Books
- HowExpert.com/courses – HowExpert Courses
- HowExpert.com/clothing – HowExpert Clothing
- HowExpert.com/membership – HowExpert Membership Site
- HowExpert.com/affiliates – HowExpert Affiliate Program
- HowExpert.com/jobs – HowExpert Jobs
- HowExpert.com/writers – Write About Your #1 Passion/Knowledge/Expertise & Become a HowExpert Author.
- HowExpert.com/resources – Additional HowExpert Recommended Resources
- YouTube.com/HowExpert – Subscribe to HowExpert YouTube.
- Instagram.com/HowExpert – Follow HowExpert on Instagram.
- Facebook.com/HowExpert – Follow HowExpert on Facebook.

Publisher's Foreword

Dear HowExpert Reader,

HowExpert publishes quick 'how to' guides on all topics from A to Z by everyday experts.

At HowExpert, our mission is to discover, empower, and maximize everyday people's talents to ultimately make a positive impact in the world for all topics from A to Z...one everyday expert at a time!

All of our HowExpert guides are written by everyday people just like you and me, who have a passion, knowledge, and expertise for a specific topic.

We take great pride in selecting everyday experts who have a passion, real-life experience in a topic, and excellent writing skills to teach you about the topic you are also passionate about and eager to learn.

We hope you get a lot of value from our HowExpert guides, and it can make a positive impact on your life in some way. All of our readers, including you, help us continue living our mission of positively impacting the world for all spheres of influences from A to Z.

If you enjoyed one of our HowExpert guides, then please take a moment to send us your feedback from wherever you got this book.

Thank you, and we wish you all the best in all aspects of life.

Sincerely,

BJ Min
Founder & Publisher of HowExpert
HowExpert.com

PS...If you are also interested in becoming a HowExpert author, then please visit our website at HowExpert.com/writers. Thank you & again, all the best!

COPYRIGHT, LEGAL NOTICE AND DISCLAIMER:

COPYRIGHT © BY HOWEXPERT™ (OWNED BY HOT METHODS). ALL RIGHTS RESERVED WORLDWIDE. NO PART OF THIS PUBLICATION MAY BE REPRODUCED IN ANY FORM OR BY ANY MEANS, INCLUDING SCANNING, PHOTOCOPYING, OR OTHERWISE WITHOUT PRIOR WRITTEN PERMISSION OF THE COPYRIGHT HOLDER.

DISCLAIMER AND TERMS OF USE: PLEASE NOTE THAT MUCH OF THIS PUBLICATION IS BASED ON PERSONAL EXPERIENCE AND ANECDOTAL EVIDENCE. ALTHOUGH THE AUTHOR AND PUBLISHER HAVE MADE EVERY REASONABLE ATTEMPT TO ACHIEVE COMPLETE ACCURACY OF THE CONTENT IN THIS GUIDE, THEY ASSUME NO RESPONSIBILITY FOR ERRORS OR OMISSIONS. ALSO, YOU SHOULD USE THIS INFORMATION AS YOU SEE FIT, AND AT YOUR OWN RISK. YOUR PARTICULAR SITUATION MAY NOT BE EXACTLY SUITED TO THE EXAMPLES ILLUSTRATED HERE; IN FACT, IT'S LIKELY THAT THEY WON'T BE THE SAME, AND YOU SHOULD ADJUST YOUR USE OF THE INFORMATION AND RECOMMENDATIONS ACCORDINGLY.

THE AUTHOR AND PUBLISHER DO NOT WARRANT THE PERFORMANCE, EFFECTIVENESS OR APPLICABILITY OF ANY SITES LISTED OR LINKED TO IN THIS BOOK. ALL LINKS ARE FOR INFORMATION PURPOSES ONLY AND ARE NOT WARRANTED FOR CONTENT, ACCURACY OR ANY OTHER IMPLIED OR EXPLICIT PURPOSE.

ANY TRADEMARKS, SERVICE MARKS, PRODUCT NAMES OR NAMED FEATURES ARE ASSUMED TO BE THE PROPERTY OF THEIR RESPECTIVE OWNERS, AND ARE USED ONLY FOR REFERENCE. THERE IS NO IMPLIED ENDORSEMENT IF WE USE ONE OF THESE TERMS.

NO PART OF THIS BOOK MAY BE REPRODUCED, STORED IN A RETRIEVAL SYSTEM, OR TRANSMITTED BY ANY OTHER MEANS: ELECTRONIC, MECHANICAL, PHOTOCOPYING, RECORDING, OR OTHERWISE, WITHOUT THE PRIOR WRITTEN PERMISSION OF THE AUTHOR.

ANY VIOLATION BY STEALING THIS BOOK OR DOWNLOADING OR SHARING IT ILLEGALLY WILL BE PROSECUTED BY LAWYERS TO THE FULLEST EXTENT. THIS PUBLICATION IS PROTECTED UNDER THE US COPYRIGHT ACT OF 1976 AND ALL OTHER APPLICABLE INTERNATIONAL, FEDERAL, STATE AND LOCAL LAWS AND ALL RIGHTS ARE RESERVED, INCLUDING RESALE RIGHTS: YOU ARE NOT ALLOWED TO GIVE OR SELL THIS GUIDE TO ANYONE ELSE.

THIS PUBLICATION IS DESIGNED TO PROVIDE ACCURATE AND AUTHORITATIVE INFORMATION WITH REGARD TO THE SUBJECT MATTER COVERED. IT IS SOLD WITH THE UNDERSTANDING THAT THE AUTHORS AND PUBLISHERS ARE NOT ENGAGED IN RENDERING LEGAL, FINANCIAL, OR OTHER PROFESSIONAL ADVICE. LAWS AND PRACTICES OFTEN VARY FROM STATE TO STATE AND IF LEGAL OR OTHER EXPERT ASSISTANCE IS REQUIRED, THE SERVICES OF A PROFESSIONAL SHOULD BE SOUGHT. THE AUTHORS AND PUBLISHER SPECIFICALLY DISCLAIM ANY LIABILITY THAT IS INCURRED FROM THE USE OR APPLICATION OF THE CONTENTS OF THIS BOOK.

COPYRIGHT BY HOWEXPERT™ (OWNED BY HOT METHODS)
ALL RIGHTS RESERVED WORLDWIDE.

Table of Contents

Recommended Resources 2

Publisher's Foreword 3

Introduction 6

Chapter 1: Takedowns, takedown defense, and movement 10

Chapter 2: Standing in guard. 47

Chapter 3: Escapes 57

Chapter 4: Sweeps 74

Chapter 5: Attacks from guard 85

Chapter 6: Attacks from mount 104

Chapter 7: Putting it together 117

Chapter 8: Cross training with standup attacks and defense 120

Conclusion 131

Author the Expert 132

Recommended Resources 133

Introduction

Jiu-jitsu is a martial art. Applications for jiu-jitsu are found in self-defense, jiu-jitsu competitions, and mixed martial arts competitions. Primary aspects of jiu-jitsu are defense, sweeps, chokes, and limb locks. It is designed to allow a smaller opponent to defeat a larger opponent. A jiu-jitsu practitioner and teacher once said, "nobody's a tough guy when they can't breathe". This idea is the premise of jiu-jitsu in that it identifies that even the toughest person has a weak spot and can be defeated.

Jiu-jitsu origins are debated. Some say it was developed in India by monks, while others trace origins back to Japan. Both histories may be true. The most popular form of modern jiu-jitsu is Brazilian jiu-jitsu. Brazilian jiu-jitsu was created by the Gracie family and has been passed down the family lineage since the time of Helio Gracie. In 1998, Gracie jiu-jitsu gained wide-spread popularity after being showcased at Ultimate Fighting Championship 1. At UFC1 Royce Gracie defeated bigger, stronger opponents using Gracie jiu-jitsu. From there jiu-jitsu has gained popularity and new offshoots of jiu-jitsu have emerged or been brought into the spotlight.

Jiu-jitsu is a very complex and technical form of combat. Arguably, it is more technical than any other form of martial arts. For example, in boxing, kickboxing, or any other similar form of martial arts, a knockout punch can still be a knockout punch even if it is off center. A choke or limb-lock is different. A choke has to be placed just right or it does not work. It might hurt but it will not cause the opponent to lose consciousness. For that reason, the moves described have to be done just right. Due to this, it can take more time to learn jiu-jitsu because of the level of technical skill required.

Jiu-jitsu is often referred to as ground game. While the ground is a large aspect of jiu-jitsu, it is not all that jiu-jitsu encompasses. Many jiu-jitsu techniques are employed while standing. Chokes, locks, defense, and takedowns can all be performed from a standing position. We will cover aspects for both the standing and ground based areas of jiu-jitsu.

In this manual, the basics of jiu-jitsu for self-defense application will be covered. Defensive maneuvers will be a primary focus, as that is the first part of any good jiu-jitsu program. The ability to defend against a larger or more skilled opponent is essential to preventing the fight from being taken to the ground or in surviving a fight when it is goes to the ground. Seven specific areas will be covered.

1. Takedowns, takedown defense, and movement – this will relay movement, some basic takedowns, and how to defend against them.

2. Standing in guard – this will detail basic defense against an opponent who pushes or knocks you to the ground yet stays standing.

3. Escapes – this will show how to move from a submissive position to a dominant position on the ground by using basic escapes.

4. Sweeps – similar to the Escapes section, this will detail how to move from a submissive position to a dominant position using basic sweeps.

5. Attacks from guard – closed guard is one of the greatest defensive and offensive positions for a person on their back. This section will offer a few key attacks and chains for defending off your back.

6. Attacks from mount – this will show you how to control and attack from the top mount once you have achieved it.

7. Putting it together – this section will show you how to chain some of these movements together.

An eighth area will be included that covers a brief introduction to stand–up striking in the form of boxing. All fights start standing. A good defense and offense will help you in this position to control the fight and avoid damage. There will be some content overlap in the sections, as they are all interrelated.

Safety first

Before moving on, it is important to take a moment to consider safety. Be mindful of the following points:

•Always practice safety first. When practicing any form of martial art or engaging in any strenuous activity, the possibility of injury is present. For this reason, it is necessary to be mindful of safety practices to limit the number of bumps, bruises, and injuries that occur, as well as minimizing the severity.

•These moves are hard to practice alone. A grappling dummy can be used, but a good training partner is better. Find a partner who will work well with you. A good partner helps you learn the moves. They do not try to make it a fight. Minimal resistance is used when practicing and learning the moves. This allows the technique to develop.

•When practicing the following moves, always practice them in a safe area. Ideally, these moves should be practiced on jiu-jitsu or wrestling specific mats. Be sure that objects that could be harmful are not in the way. A takedown performed next to a cabinet could result in a bumped head, or worse.

•When practicing chokes, joint locks, strikes, or any other move, apply the minimum amount of pressure needed to perform the moves. Practice is to learn, not hurt.

•Grappling is the sparring of jiu-jitsu. It is when the training partners actively try to perform the moves on the other person. During grappling sessions, opponent resistance is increased so pressure will be increased, yet there is still the need to be mindful of how much pressure is applied. Only apply enough pressure to successfully complete the move or get the opponent to tap.

I want to cover one final note about the manual before we begin. As you work through various moves, you will notice that I refer to you as the defender and your opponent as the attacker. The moves you use will enable you to defend against the attacker. However, the moves the attacker uses are moves you should learn as well. They are moves that can be useful to both parties. For example, one of the first moves you are going to defend against is the double leg takedown. Being able to defend against this move will help you stop a person from taking you to the ground and doing harm. The double leg can be useful for you to attack with as well. At some point in a fight, you might feel the desire to take the fight to the ground, ideally in an attempt to incapacitate your attacker to protect yourself. In this case, a double leg could be useful. Besides the moves being useful, they are fun to learn as well. So as you and your partner work through this manual, take turns playing the defender and the attacker so that both of you can learn all of the moves.

Chapter 1: Takedowns, takedown defense, and movement

All fights start standing. The best way to avoid a being taken to the ground is to avoid a fight altogether. Proper communication and other non-violent, non-aggressive steps should first be taken to avoid a fight whenever possible. The second way to avoid the takedown, and potentially the fight too, is to keep distance between yourself and the aggressor, then leaving the scene as soon as possible. However, that is not always possible.

When a fight has initiated, the best way to avoid damage from strikes, and avoid going to the ground, is to use evasive maneuvers. The most basic of these is "keeping the distance". This is a common term used in any martial arts. "Keeping the distance" refers to maintaining the distance between yourself and an opponent. The distance required will vary on your, or the aggressor's, intent.

To avoid strikes and takedowns, a good rule of thumb is to keep a double arms' length distance from the attacker. This means if you are standing in-stance and extended your front arm straight out and the aggressor did the same, you would not touch hands. **Refer to the strikes section for proper stance**. This is a good distance for safety since an aggressor who cannot reach you cannot hurt you. This double arm lengths distance is good for avoiding kicks as well as punches. A double arms' length is longer than the average person's leg. A person at the distance will not be able to hit you without first closing the distance. This applies to takedowns as well.

From a double arms' length distance, a person will need to close the distance to perform a takedown. The further the attacker is from the defender, the longer it will take the attacker to close the distance and achieve the takedown. This increased time will allow the defender to see the attacker attempting the takedown and allow the defender to use a takedown defense or counter. Whenever possible, keep the distance. If the aggressor moves toward you, you step back. If you cannot step back, then circle out. This type of movement is part of basic footwork taught in stand up striking forms of combat such as boxing or kickboxing.

What is a takedown?

A takedown is a move that an attacker will use to get the defender to the ground. Takedown defense refers to a move that the defender uses to stop the attacker from taking them to the ground. When a counter is applied to an attacker attempting a takedown, the defender is using an attacking move to counter the takedown. In the following section, you will be the defender and the other person will be the attacker.

Double leg takedown, tackle, defense, and counters.

One of the most basic takedowns is also one that is most likely to be employed in the streets. It is the double leg takedown or tackle. The double leg takedown is a wrestling move that relies on the attacker bending at the knees while moving toward the defender, grabbing behind the knees, and pushing forward with the shoulder and head pressed into the stomach or waist area of the defender. The tackle is basically the same thing, except the attacker generally grips the defender around the waist. This is more common in the street by an unskilled opponent. There are defenses and counters to both moves. The defenses and counters outlined in the following section will refer directly to the double leg takedown, but are equally applicable to a tackle. The following series of pictures will outline the double leg takedown and the tackle.

Double Leg Takedown

Figure 1: This is the start position for the double leg takedown. The attacker and defender are face to face. While the body

positions/stances may vary slightly from situation to situation, the double leg will always be achieved from a frontal attack.

Figure 2: The attacker will move in on the defender. The attacker will lower himself or herself, also known as changing levels. The attacker will put himself or herself at about waist height, grab behind the defender's knees, and place their shoulder in the defender's stomach.

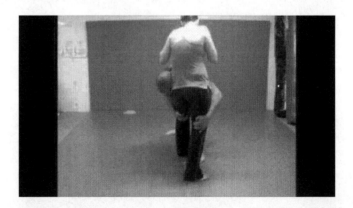

Figure 3: This is a rear shot of the same position. Notice the hand placement of the attacker's hands behind the defender's legs and the placement of the attacker's shoulder in the defender's stomach.

Figure 4: From this position, the attacker will drive forward into the defender's stomach while pulling the knees of the defender into the attacker. This will drive the defender's body backwards while making them unable to balance.

Figure 5: The attacker pushes forward.

Figure 6: The attacker has successfully taken down the defender.

Tackle

Figure 7: The start position for the tackle.

Figure 8: For the tackle, the attacker is a bit higher on the defender's body. The attacker gets a hold on the defender at about waist height.

Figure 9: The rear view of the same position.

Figure 10: From this position, the attacker drives forward, relying on the momentum alone to force the defender to lose balance and fall to the ground.

Figure 11: The attacker drives forward.

Figure 12: The attacker has successfully taken the defender down

The **double leg takedown** and **tackle** have multiple defenses and counters. Only a few will be covered here. The first is the **head push and pivot**. The following series of images will outline it.

Push And Pivot Defense

Figure 13: This is the beginning position for the head push and pivot

Figure 14: In this picture, the attacker moves in for the takedown. The defender extends her hand toward the attacker's head.

Figure 15: As the attacker moves forward, the defender pushes away on the attacker's head and pivots to the side of the defending arm.

Figure 16: The defender is out of the way of the attacker's line of motion. From here, the defender can step away, throw a punch to the attacker's head, or throw another strike at the attacker.

Figure 17: This is the opposite side view of the finishing position. From here, you can see how easy it would be to step away or throw a strike, especially with the defender's rear hand.

The head push is one of my favorite defensive moves to a rushing opponent. It can be used from multiple angles and heights. The above is the first example, but it can also be used for someone who is going for a head grab. In this case, instead of pushing the head, I push the face, but the idea is the same. I still push the person's head/face away and pivot away from them. The head or face push is useful from so many positions. On the ground, a person can create space using the head or face push. The same is true for the clinch. Therefore, as you are practicing these moves and committing them to memory, stop from time to time and think about how these moves and others can be utilized from different positions. A move is only a bad idea if it does not work. If it works, go for it!

The next double leg defense is the shoulder stop. It can be done with the **palms (shoulder-palm stop)** or with the **forearms (forearm-shoulder stop)**. The next series of images will outline both.

Palm-Shoulder Stop

Figure 18: This is the start position for the palm shoulder stop.

Figure 19: The attacker moves in. As he does, the defender steps one foot back and extends the arms toward the attacker.

Figure 20: The defender has put her palms on the attacker to stop the defender's forward motion. It is important to put the rear leg and arms out far enough to apply the same amount of pressure or more as the attacker. The defender in this image uses this stance but others may want to put the rear leg further back and extend the arms more. It is a personal preference but it should allow the defender (you) to comfortably balance and apply enough counter pressure to stop the attacker's forward movement.

Figure 21: In this image, you can see that the attacker cannot get a firm grasp on the defender's body or legs. This is the point. The defender can widen this gap by stepping further back with the leg and extending the arms more.

Forearm-Shoulder Stop

Figure 22: This is the start position for the forearm stop.

Figure 23: The attacker moves forward in the same a manner as palm-shoulder stop. This time the defender uses her forearms to stop the forward movement. All the same dynamic principals apply here. The only real difference in this move is the use of the forearms and the fact that it is better for a closer opponent or an opponent who moves in at a higher shoulder level.

The elbow stop is one of my favorite defenses for a rushing opponent. I do a one armed variation most of the time. The way I do this is by using just my forward arm to shoulder stop the opponent. My free hand does not just hang around though. I can do a few things with the free hand. I can work for an underhook on the opponent's arm with the free hand, look for an attack, or push the opponent's head toward to the ground. Pushing the head toward the ground can cause the attacker to become off balance and fall. The head push alone could be enough, but when combined with the attacker's forward momentum this can be done even more easily when properly applied. Attacks such as a number of chokes or strikes can be set up from here as well. Finally, the underhook can be used to give me control over the person's body that I can use for a number of purposes.

The final defense to the double leg takedown is the **guillotine choke**, a popular jiu-jitsu move that has moved over to MMA. It is a bit harder to pull off, which is why the guillotine choke is listed last. It is similar to the previous two defenses with one exception. Instead of shoulder stopping the attacker, the defender slips one arm around the attacker's neck to sink in a choke. While this is a defense, it can commonly be referred to as a counter, which is the more appropriate term. This choke can be used to counter from a standing position (**standing guillotine choke**) and as the attacker completes the takedown (**standard guillotine choke**). (**Note**: the guillotine can be applied from other positions as well but we will not be outlining those here.) The following photos will outline both the **standing guillotine choke** and **standard guillotine choke**.

Gullotine Choke Counter

Figure 24: This is the start position for the standing guillotine choke. As was mentioned, the guillotine choke is applied as a counter-attacker in this situation.

Figure 25: The attacker moves in for the takedown. At this point, the defender can do a few things. First, she can stand right in front and attempt to catch the attackers head for the move. Second, she can step to the side to allow the attackers head to line up for the move. Third, the defender can push the attacker's head to the side as he moves forward in order to move the head in line for the move. Finally, the attacker can step slightly to the side and push the attacker's head to line it up for the move. Any of these set-ups will work as long as the attacker's head ends up in the correct position. It is a matter of personal preference and situation. Time and practice will help you learn which works better for you.

Figure 26: The defender shoots her arm around the attacker's neck. She reaches the choking hand around to the other side of her body where she clasps both hands together. The choke does not generally go in perfectly immediately. The inside of the elbow needs to be lined up with the front of the attacker's throat. From the current position, the defender can adjust the arm position until the choke is sunk in.

Figure 27: Notice how the hands are clasped together. The defender has reached her arm around the attacker's neck to the other side and joined hands. The stance she has is a little wider than shoulder width and her knees are slightly bent. Different hand grips can be used. Palm-to-palm, inverted palm-to-palm, and palm-to-wrist are my preferred grips. Experiment with grips to see which one you like best. As long as you are able to perform the move properly, the grip does not matter.

Figure 28: The guillotine in more detail. Notice the arm that is extended. It is the choking arm.

Figure 29: The arm reaches downward, preparing to slide under the throat.

Figure 30: The arm is extended under the neck, the inner elbow goes under the throat, and the arm reaches to the other side of the body.

Figure 31: The choking arm is connected with the hand of the non-choking arm. Different grips can be used here. As long as you can perform the choke, any grip is fine.

Figure 32: Lift on the neck by pushing the shoulder blades backward and pushing the pelvis slightly forward. Keep a bend in your knees. Do not try to stand tall. For safety purposes, during practice do not push the shoulders back all the way or push the pelvis completely forward. This would sink the choke in deep and could seriously hurt your training partner. In a real situation, you would push the shoulders back and pelvis forward. You would essentially create a dip in your lower back that allows you to lift the opponent's neck. In an extreme situation, the opponent may even be lifted off the ground. In practice, exercise caution.

Figure 33: In the event that the defender is unable to stop the attacker from moving forward, you can maintain the guillotine to the ground and choke the attacker out there.

Figure 34: As the attacker keeps pushing forward the defender needs to keep a firm grip on the neck of the attacker. Allow yourself to fall in a controlled manner with the momentum. Remember, this is only if you cannot stop the attacker from moving forward. Do not go to the ground on your back unless forced.

Figure 35: As the defender falls to the ground, she wraps her legs around the attacker to establish guard. Notice how she keeps her head high. This will help prevent the head from hitting the ground. While this type of hit could knock you out, it could also just cause you to lose your grip on the neck or guard.

Figure 36: The defender is now on the ground but she has a firm grip on the attacker's neck and body. From here the defender can choke the attacker out or hurt/hold him until she can mount a sweep or escape.

Figure 37: Side view of the last frame.

Figure 38: Opposite side view of the last frame.

The body-fold takedown, ankle trip takedown, defense, and counters

The next two takedowns are accomplished once the attacker has control of the defender's waist. This position is also known as a "**body clinch**". They are the two more common takedowns seen in the streets. The first is the **body fold takedown** and the second is the **ankle trip takedown**. The next series of pictures will outline these.

Body-Fold Takedown

Figure 39: This is the start position for the body fold takedown.

Figure 40: The attacker achieves the body clinch.

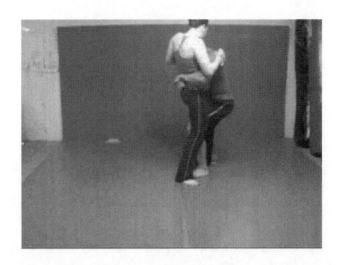

Figure 41: From this position, the attacker will lower their body slightly and stay in tight on the defender's body.

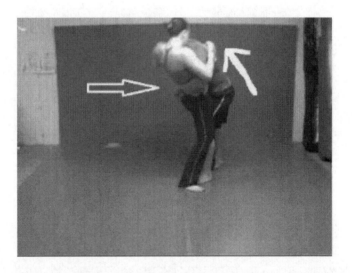

Figure 42: The attacker will then push upward and forward with their shoulder while pulling the defender's body toward them with the body clinch. See arrows.

Figure 43: This movement pushes the defender off balance and they will begin to fall backwards.

Figure 44: The attacker follows the defender to the ground and lands in a dominant position such as in-guard.

Leg-Hook Takedown

Figure 45: This is the start position for the leg-hook takedown.

Figure 46: The attacker closes the distance and establishes a body-clinch on the defender.

Figure 47: The attacker places on of his feet behind the foot of the defender to act as a tripping mechanism. The attacker's foot may simply be used to trip or the attacker may use the foot to hook and pull the defenders foot of the ground. Both are common ways this takedown is employed.

Figure 48: The attacker pushes forward effectively tripping the defender...

Figure 49: which causes them to lose balance and fall to the ground.

Figure 50: The attacker is now in a dominant position (mount) and can do damage to the defender.

The defenses to the both of these techniques are essentially the same. The first defense is to prevent the attacker from getting into the position to complete these move. Keeping the distance is the best way to do this but the **head-push and pivot** and **shoulder-stop** moves are effective here. If the attacker gets a grip on the defender's waist, then there are a few more options from which to choose. The first step is to **step back with the feet and create**

space between the defender's body and the attacker's body. The **body-fold takedown** and **leg-hook takedown** rely on the attacker being close to the defender. The more space between the attacker and the defender, the harder the takedown is to complete for the attacker. The next series of pictures will outline how the defender can create space between them and the attacker. These pictures will also outline how to use what is referred to as "**snaking**" and how to incorporate **punches as a counter**.

Step Back And Create Space

Figure 51: If an attacker has established a body-clinch, the first thing to do is to create space.

Figure 52: In this image, the defender has taken a step back with her right foot. She has placed it behind her in a strong position to establish a solid base. From here, she can push forward with her body to stop the forward movement of the attacker. This also creates space to set up strikes or other maneuvers.

Throwing A Punch

Figure 53: While maintaining the space, the defender pulls back her right arm to deliver a blow to the attacker's body.

Figure 54: The defender delivers a blow to the attacker's stomach. Blows can be delivered to the any part of the body that is accessible but delivering a blow to the ribs or stomach is likely to be most effective. A strong body blow to the stomach can cause shortness of breath in the attacker. An attacker that cannot breathe cannot effectively attack. Pain will also occur because of a blow to the stomach or ribs. This may be enough to discourage an attacker from pushing forward. Ideally, this will encourage the attacker to separate from the defender. At the very least, it will stall the attacker and allow the defender to move into an attack such as more punches, the guillotine, or snake arms defense.

Snake Arms

Figure 55: This is the start position for snake arms. For this move, the defender creates space between herself and the attacker. She then snakes her arms inside his to move into a more dominant double underhook position.

Figure 56: The defender takes her hand and moves it toward the inside of the attackers arm. The intent is to shoot the arm inside of the attacker's grip.

Figure 57: The defender has moved her hand inside and through the attacker's grip.

Figure 58: The defender has now achieved what is known as an underhook with the snaking arm. Having the arm under the attacker's armpit is a stronger position than having arms over the attackers shoulder.

Figure 59: Now the defender wants to achieve and under hook on the opposite side.

Figure 60: same as with the opposite side, the defender works her arm through the attackers grip.

Figure 61: She underhooks the attacker's body on this side. She now has double underhooks.

Figure 62: There are a number of techniques possible from this position. In this case, defender's desire is to get away so she uses the double underhooks to put her hands on the attacker's chest. From here she pushes off the attacker.

Figure 63: The defender has pushed herself off the attacker and stepped away.

Figure 64: The defender moves into her striking stance.

In this section you have learned:

1. What a takedown is.

2. How to perform a takedown.

3. How to defend against a takedown.

4. How to counter a takedown.

You are ready to learn techniques for standing in guard.

Chapter 2: Standing in guard.

What I want to cover in this section is standing in guard. An attacker may push you to the ground or punch you hard enough to knock you to the ground. If you are incapacitated by the punch then there is not much you can do. If the punch only knocks you to the ground, there are some options.

Ideally, you want to get up as fast as possible. However, this may not be possible. If the attacker is far enough away, then you want to get up. "Far enough away" would be a distance where you can get to your feet with minimal risk of him or her rushing and punching, kicking, or tackling you to the ground. The optimal range for this is if the person is far enough away when you kick with your feet parallel to the ground that you cannot reach them. You could then get up. Just as important as making sure the attacker is far enough away is knowing how to get up correctly.

When getting up you do not want to take you eyes off the attacker. You *Always* want to be able to see what the attacker is doing. Second, you want to get up in an explosive manner. Getting up slowly increases the chance the person will be able to rush. Third, you want to get up in a stable base, which is referred to as **getting up in base**. That will be covered shortly.

If you cannot safely get up, you have options. The first thing to understand is to not freak out. Freaking out is your enemy. Stay controlled and focused. Next, put your legs up as if you are in the guard position, which we will detail more later.From here, you can do a few things. The first is using your **legs in defense**.

Legs In Defense

Figure 65: Legs in defense is essentially how it sounds. The defender uses her legs to keep the attacker at a distance.

Figure 66: As the attacker moves around the defender looking to mount an attack, the defender circles with him. If the attacker moves to one side, the defender puts the leg on the same side to the ground. The defender uses this foot to move in the same direction as the attacker. She keeps the other foot up. If the attacker moves forward, one foot is already up in defense. She simply needs to bring the second up.

Figure 67: The defender follows the attacker.

Figure 68: The defender follows the attacker.

An attacker is likely not going to stay outside of your guard for too long. He or she is going to want to get past you legs and attack you. An attacker may come straight down the middle. If they do, stop their forward movement with your legs by placing your feet on their hips. From here, you can do a few things, depending on if they are leaning heavily on your legs or just lightly. If the attacker is leaning heavily on your legs, you can pull them into guard, which will be covered as part of the punch block series. If the attacker is leaning lightly, then you can take them down using the hook- pick takedown.

Hook-Pick Takedown

Figure 69: The attacker is looking to move in on the defender. He is being kept back be her feet on his hips. He is not leaning hard enough to be pulled into guard (punch-block defense), so the defender looks to take the attacker down.

Figure 70: The defender does three things at once to set up this move. She grabs the attacker's forward ankle with her hand, hooks his far leg with her far foot, and presses her other foot into the attacker's hip.

Figure 71: The defender then pushes the attacker with the foot on the hip, pulls the attacker's far leg that she has hooked with her foot, and pulls on the attacker's ankle that she is gripping with her hand.

Figure 72: The attacker is now on the ground. The defender can get up in base safely.

Getting Up In Base

The following images will show how to get up in base using one hand to balance on. The other hand is kept up in defense against the attacker in order to protect the face. Two hands on the ground generally will allow a person to get up in base easier as well as quicker. Two hands combined with a kind of "pop" up or little hop up will get a person up even quicker. I prefer the two handed version, but it is important to know the one handed version. Try both. The two handed version is the same as below with the exception that you place both hands on the mat or ground.

Figure 73: Getting up in base is essential for the attacker to safely get from the ground and back to her feet. The defender starts in the back position with her guard up.

Figure 74: The defender posts up on her arm. To defend against the attacker the defender keeps the opposite arm up in defense.

Figure 75: The defender slides her bottom leg back so that her legs are in proper stance.

Figure 76: The defender stands up in base. From here, she can look to attack with strikes, a takedown of her own, or put space between herself and the attacker.

Shin Kick To Get Up

If the attacker is standing in guard but is not close enough for the hook-pick takedown, or to be pulled into the guard, then the defender can use the shin kick to get up.

Figure 77: For this series of images, the role of attacker and defender will be reversed. The defender is on his back on the ground. His legs are up in defense. The attacker is standing in guard.

Figure 78: The defender kicks the attacker in the shin. The purpose of this is to get the attacker to step back.

Figure 79: The defender kicks the attacker until she steps back enough for the defender to perform the get-up.

Figure 80: The defender kicks one last time to make sure there is enough space. He posts up on his elbow at the same time.

Figure 81: The defender slides his leg back while popping up on his hand. He moves his leg into base.

Figure 82: The defender stands up in base and sets himself in the proper stance to defend.

Double the learning

In the preceding section, I have introduced you to the basic stand up attacks and defense. The primary goal of this section was to teach you how to defend the various takedowns and a couple of other standing attacks. However, as I mentioned at the start of this manual, you should also be able to learn the attacks that you are defending against. You and your partner should switch back and forth between being the defender and the attacker. This will allow you to learn both the attacking and defending aspects of the section.

A Quick Review

In this section you have learned:

5. What standing in guard means.

6. How to use legs in defense.

7. How to defend against an opponent standing in guard.

8. How to take down an opponent standing in guard.

9. How to get up on base.

Chapter 3: Escapes

In the previous section, I illustrated how to avoid, defend, and attack off takedowns. This section will cover what to do if the attacker takes you to the ground and has you on your back. The first thing I want to do is describe some of the different jiu-jitsu positions when on the ground. These positions will apply to this section and the following section. The following series of photos will layout the different positions we will cover.

Figure 83: In this photo, the attacker (in blue) is in full-mount top while the defender is in full-mount bottom. The attacker is utilizing a high-mount, which is with the attacker knees pushed into the defender's armpits. This is a great attacking position for punches, certain chokes, and certain arm locks.

Figure 84: In this image, the attacker and defender are in the same basic positions as the previous frame. This time the attacker

is utilizing a low mount with his hands posted out (placed on the mat). This is a good control position that can set up for attacks as well.

Figure 85: In this position, the attacker is in-guard top with the defender in-guard bottom. A person is in-guard whenever they find themselves in this position. This is the best position for a defender to be in if they are on their back. From here, the defender can move toward getting up, defending, and attacking.

Figure 86: In this image, the defender has a closed guard on the attacker who is in guard. Closed-guard and in-guard are two common positions. This is a strong position for the defender who is on her back. From this position sweeps, strikes, locks, and chokes can be set up.

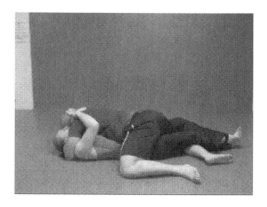

Figure 87: This position is half-guard. The defender has only one of the attacker's legs tied up, which equals half-guard. The defender is in half-guard bottom with the attacker in half guard top. There are different variations of half-guard.

Figure 88: This is one type of side-control position. There are multiple side-control positions. In this image, the attacker is in side-mount top with head and arm control, while the defender is in side-mount bottom.

Some people feel that being on ones back is the worst position in a fight. While this may be the truth, there is a lot that a person can do off their back in jiu-jitsu. There are joint locks attacks, chokes, sweeps, and defensive techniques. A person can also choose to employ strikes, although they are not generally a part of traditional jiu-jitsu. However, unless you are in a grappling only setting, knowing how to use strikes from the bottom is essential. In this manual, you will learn to use strikes from multiple positions. Before we get to strikes, or any attacks, I will show you how to defend yourself from strikes and jiu-jitsu attacks. I will again refer to you as the defender and the other person as the attacker.

Defense by controlling the attacker: wrist control, head control, and closed guard

When fighting off the back (bottom position) the defender must control the movements and posture of the attacker in top position. Ideally, if the defender is on their back, the best place for the attacker to be is in-guard. From here, the defender can better control the attacker and defend against strikes or other attacks while looking for an opportunity to sweep or attack. The best way to control an opponent is to control their posture. The defender wants to keep the attack close to them so that the attacker cannot get the space required to throw punches, try to pass, or attack with a choke or joint lock. The way to do this is for the attacker to close their guard on the attacker and establish head control.

Figure 89: In this image, the attacker has successfully taken the defender down. The attacker is inside of the defender's open guard. The defender seeks to establish control of the attacker.

Figure 90: The defender keeps her hand in high position. She raises her feet off the ground.

Figure 91: The defender closes her legs around the attacker. Her guard is still in high position.

Figure 92: Side view of closed guard.

Figure 93: Rear view from closed guard.

Figure 94: The defender now seeks to establish head control. She reaches her arms up and around the attackers head.

Figure 95: The defender now has head control on the attacker in the closed guard position. The position of the hands and arms can

vary greatly here. In the above image, the defender has looped on arm around the head of the attacker. With the other hand, she has gripped the arm around the attacker. This is a fine position, but there are other options as well. Experiment with hand and arm positions and grips to see what a strong control position is for you.

If the attacker does posture up (sit up) and create distance, then it becomes important to control the attacker's arms. This is done using wrist control, which is essentially grabbing hold of the attacker's wrist and controlling their arms in this manner. Wrist control can be done in any position by both the attacker and defender. The next image illustrates just a single example.

Figure 96: Wrist control in guard. By controlling the wrist, the defender can prevent the attacker from punching, passing, or other maneuvers.

Elbow Escape From Mount

If the attacker achieves mount, you want to get out of this position as quick as possible. The best way to do this is with a sweep or escape. The elbow escape is a common and effective escape utilized by jiu-jitsu practitioners.

Figure 97: For this series of images, the role of attacker and defender will again be reversed. The attacker (pink shirt) is in full mount. The defender (blue shirt) has his hands clasped behind the back of the attacker to control her posture.

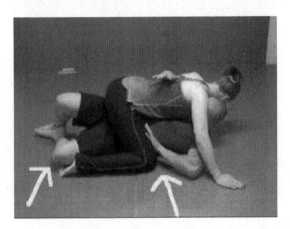

Figure 98: The defender slides his knee on one side toward the ground. The defender quickly moves one hand to the knee of the attacker.

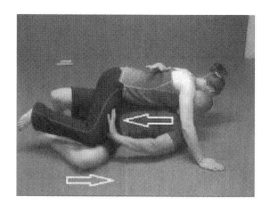

Figure 99: The defender pushes the attackers knee away and up while sliding his same side knee under the attacker's leg. Since his leg is lying on its side, this allows the knee and leg to move under the attacker's leg with ease.

Figure 100: The defender hooks his leg on the inside of the attacker's leg to hold it in place. He secures control of her arm. This keeps control of the attacker so she is not able to improve her position and allows the defender to perform the rest of the elbow escape on the opposite side.

Figure 101: This is the opposite side view. The defender is controlling the attacker.

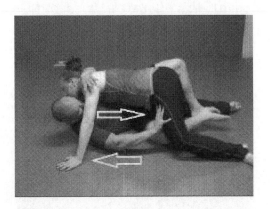

Figure 102: The defender again pushes the knee of the attacker down and up while again sliding his leg under the attacker's knee.

Figure 103: In this position, the defender now has one butterfly guard. This means his shin is placed on the inside of the attacker's

leg. This is normal. To complete the escape on this side the defender adds an extra step.

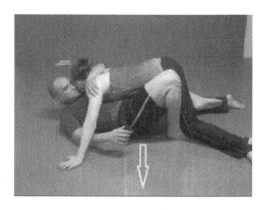

Figure 104: The free the butterfly guard, the defender pushes his hips to the side where he wants to free the hook (see the direction of the arrow). This begins to slide his leg free and moves him into a position where he can completely free his leg.

Figure 105: The defender now moves his leg into closed guard and establishes a lockdown on the attackers head. From here, he can work for moves such as the trap-and-roll sweep, armbar from guard, or others.

Elbow Escape From Half-Guard

Figure 106: The elbow escape from half-guard is another common escape. It starts with the defender having control of the attacker.

Figure 107: The defender gets his elbow between him and the attacker to create space.

Figure 108: The defender pushes up on the attacker while scooting his hips out away from the attacker to slide his leg out from under the attacker.

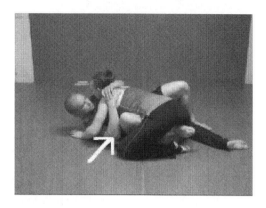

Figure 109: This is the opposite side view of the last frame. We will continue from here. Notice the position of the knee on the inside that the defender is using for butterfly guard.

Figure 110: The defender hooks his leg on the back of the attacker. He can use this and the butterfly guard to control the attacker's body. This is known as ¾ guard. The defender turn his hips toward the direction of the butterfly guard to straighten his body out.

Figure 111: The defender moves his hips toward the direction of the butterfly guard. He does this in order to free up the trapped foot.

Figure 112: Once the defender has his leg free he brings it around to the attacker's back and locks both legs together in the closed guard.

Elbow Escape From Side Control

Figure 113: The defender starts on the bottom with the attacker in side control.

Figure 114: The defender turns to push his hips out from the attacker.

Figure 115: The defender pushes his bottom knee into the opening on the side of the attacker.

Figure 116: The defender hooks the back of the attacker with his far leg. He uses it and his arms to pull himself under the attacker. He is in three-quarter guard.

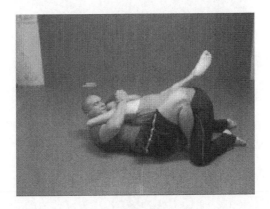

Figure 117: The defender pushes his hips toward the trapped foot to create room to free his foot.

Figure 118: With his foot free, the defender now brings the foot to the back of the attacker and closes his guard.

A Quick Review:

In this section you have learned:

1. Basic jiu-jitsu ground positions.

2. The importance of controlling an opponent.

3. How to control the opponent's body to minimize their attacking ability.

4. How to use the elbow escape from multiple positions.

5. How to get to closed guard to set up attacks and sweeps covered in section 4.

Chapter 4: Sweeps

A sweep is a technique that is used to move a person out of dominant position. A sweep is generally employed so that the defender can move into a dominant position and become the attacker. One of the basic sweeps is the trap-and-roll sweep. It goes by a number of other names depending on what teacher is instructing. The trap-and-roll sweep consists of the defender in bottom position to trap the leg and arm on one side of an attacker in mount position. The defender then bridges at an angle and rolls the attacker and themselves over so that the attacker is now on their back.

The first thing to learn in order to use the trap-and-roll sweep is how to bridge. Bridging is the act of pushing ones hips skyward in an attempt to buck off the person in top mount. Bridging can also be used for other moves but sweeping is the main use of for bridging. Bridging is always done in a skyward motion but may be done at an angle as well. Bridging skyward at an angle is necessary for completing the trap-and-roll sweep.

Bridging

Figure 119: This is essentially the start position for the trap-and-roll sweep.

Figure 120: In this image, the defender is bridging her hips skyward. This is the basic bridging motion. While there are variations to bridging, for the trap-and-roll sweep, the upper back should be on the ground, along with the feet, and the hips should be skyward.

Figure 121: This is the angled variation of the bridge. This is the movement that will be used for the trap-and-roll sweep. The angle is used so that the hips push the attacker into an off balance position and allow the defender to roll through and attain top position. You will bridge at angle toward the side you want to roll the attacker to.

Figure 122: An opposite side view of what the bridge looks like.

Figure 123: To perform the trap-and-roll sweep the defender will start in this position, but will have trapped the attacker's arm and leg. You can start with this drill for solo practice, and then practice mimicking trapping the arm and leg.

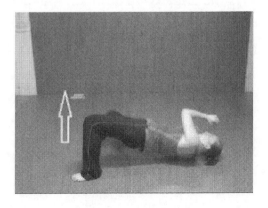

Figure 124: The defender bridges skyward at an angle.

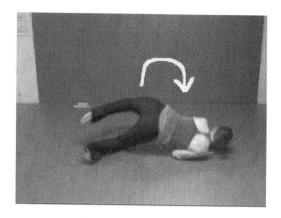

Figure 125: The defender rolls onto her knees, allowing the bottom leg to slide out and the top leg to roll over.

Figure 126: The defender lands in the mount position.

The next series of photos will show to do one variations of this move. Each variation has a time and place where it is the better move. Each one is important to learn.

Trap-And-Roll Sweep

Figure 128: This is the start position for the trap-n-roll. The attacker is in full-mount top with the defender on bottom. For illustration purposes, the hand attacker's hands are placed on the chest of the defender.

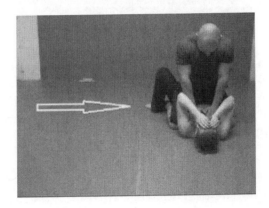

Figure 128: This is step 1 for the trap and roll. Understand that steps 1 & 2 would ideally be completed at the same time. For illustrative purposes, it is broken down in two steps. Notice the left foot of the defender. She has slipped her foot around the outside of the attacker's foot on the same side. She is effectively trapping his foot.

Figure 129: The defender has used her left hand to grab the attacker's wrist on the same side and used her right hand to grab behind his elbow. She has now trapped his arm. Ideally, this would be done with step 1. As you drill, start with two steps and try to combine them as you get better.

Figure 130: The defender now bridges at an angle while keeping the attacker's hand and foot trapped. This throws him off balance and he cannot post out (cannot put his hand or foot out to catch balance).

Figure 131: The defender follows the bridge by allowing the attacker to roll onto his back. She keeps tight with him as she rolls, being sure to maintain control.

Figure 132: The defender now has top position in-guard. From here, she has a number of options for what she can do next.

The second sweep is the elevator sweep. It is done with the attacker in guard. The next series of photos illustrate how it is performed.

Elevator Sweep

Figure 133: The elevator sweep starts with the defender on her back with the attacker in her closed guard.

Figure 134: The attacker posts one leg out as if he is going to try to posture up to throw a punch.

Figure 135: The defender scoops her leg under the attacker's extended leg.

Figure 136: This is a side view showing where the defender is scooping the attacker's leg. Notice the defender using her foot to hook the attacker's thigh. The defender will lift up on this leg to throw the attacker off balance while sweeping the opposite leg.

Figure 137: This is the opposite side view. Right now, the defender has the attacker's opposite leg hooked with her foot. From here she will lift upwards and over with her opposite foot. This drags the attacker's leg into the air and throws him off balance. The defender will sweep with the foot on this side, as noted in the image.

Figure 138: The defender is performing the elevator sweep. Notice how she is lifting the attacker's leg that she hooked and sweeping the other leg. The hooked leg gets dragged up and over while the other leg is swept under and over.

Figure 139: The defender lands in full-mount on top of the attacker. She has control of him still. From her she can base out or throw her hooks in. She could also maintain this position. Either way she would be looking to control that attacker until she felt ready to attack or get away.

A Quick Review:

In this section you have learned:

1. What a sweep is.

2. What bridging is.

3. How to bridge.

4. How to sweep an opponent.

5. How to get to top position to attack or get up.

Chapter 5: Attacks from guard

The next area to be covered is attacks from the guard. Being able to defend and attack from your back is an essential aspect of surviving a fight that is taken to the ground. Most times, when a fight ends up on the ground, the attacker ends up mounting the defender or ends up in the guard of the defender. A strong guard can neutralize punches and submissions from the attacker, while setting up attacks for the defender.

Armbar from guard

Figure 140: We now move into a traditional jiu-jitsu attack from guard: the arm bar. The defender starts with the attacker in her guard.

Figure 141: The defender grabs the wrist on the attacker's arm on the side that she wants to attack. In this case, she uses her left hand to grab the attacker wrist on the same side.

Figure 142: The defender now reaches with her right arm under the attacker's leg on her right side. She turns her body in the same direction as she does. She maintains a hold on the attacker's wrist with the other hand.

Figure 143: With the right arm, the defender has scooped her arm under the attacker's leg. She pulls her body in that direction making sure to keep a tight grip on the attacker's wrist. She allows her right leg to slide upwards.

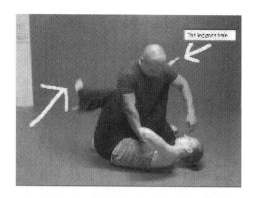

Figure 144: As the defender pulls her to the right, she swings her left leg up. The intended target for this leg is over the attackers head.

Figure 145: In this image, the defender is in proper position for the arm bar. She has control of the attackers arm. Her legs are heavy against his body and head. She pushes her hips out, similar to the bridging motion, to extend her legs and break the attacker's arm.

Figure 146: In this image, the defender is extended more. IF she were to extend further, the attackers arm would be hurt or broken. For training purposes, only extend to a slightly uncomfortable position.

Figure 147: If the attacker loses balance and falls, move with them. In this image, the attacker loses his balance and begins to fall. The defender moves with him. She keeps her legs tight to his head and body while keeping a firm grip on his arm with her hands. As the attacker falls, the defender allows his momentum to carry her with him

Figure 148: The attacker has fallen to his back. The defender follows down by allowing the momentum to pull her into a sitting position. If needed, she now scoots close to makes sure she still has the arm in the proper position. Her legs stay heavy and she keeps a firm grip on the attacker's hand.

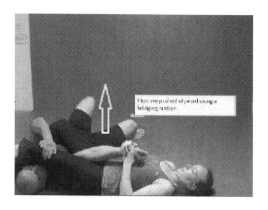

Figure 149: The defender falls back into an extended position. She pushes her hips toward the sky to apply pressure to the attackers elbow. In this image, she is not full extending. If she did so, the attacker's arm would break. In practice, come short. Only apply enough pressure for you training partner to feel it and tap. In a real fight, break the arm.

A Few More Details About The Arm Bar

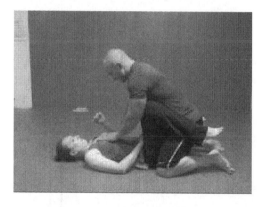

Figure 150: The arm bar can start from a few different scenarios. The attacker could be holding you down, as is shown in this image. From here, the arm bar is applied as you have already been shown.

e Figure 151: The arm bar can be used in a choking situation. The application is the same.

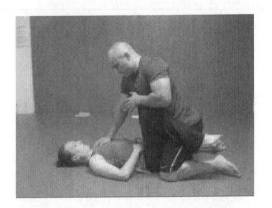

Figure 152: The attacker does not need to have both hands on you. One hand is fine. That is all you are going to attack anyway. For this reason, it is important to train the arm bar from guard on both sides. By this I mean practice attacking both arms of the attacker. This will make attacking either arm easy to achieve.

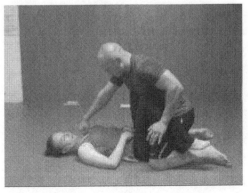

Figure 153: The arm bar can also be achieved from a punch.

Figure 154: The defender simply needs to get a hold of the punch. Practice this as well. Do so in slow motion first and not in full contact. As you and your partner become more comfortable with the moves, increase speed. I highly recommend using protective gear such as headgear and open palm striking gloves.

Figure 155: From the punch, the arm bar is completed the same. I will show it to you again, this time from the side so that you can see the specifics for the move from this angle. The defender spins to get a hold on the attacker's leg. She keeps a firm grip on the attacker's hand and allows her near leg to slide into position.

Figure 156: The defender moves her far leg into position.

Figure 157: The defender has now placed her second hand on the arm she is attacking. She is pushing her hips outward. You can see the extension in the elbow of the attacker from here. If she went any further, his arm would break.

Triangle Choke From Guard

Figure 158: The triangle choke from guard is another jiu-jitsu staple. It is one of the basic and earliest taught moves to help people defend off their back. It is a blood choke that will cause the attacker to lose consciousness in a matter of seconds when applied correctly. I would know. A 145 lb woman almost caused me to lose consciousness during practice but I tapped quickly. I am an athletic 185 lb male. This is the start position for the choke. The defender has the attacker in closed guard.

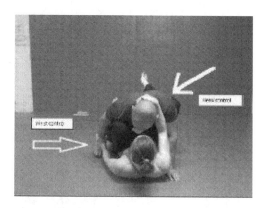

Figure 159: There are many different set-ups for this choke. These images will show you a basic set-up. After getting the move down, play around and find different ways to set it up. The defender has achieved wrist control on one arm of the attacker and has head control with the other arm.

Figure 160: The defender pulls the attackers arm away from his body. She creates enough room to slide her leg through...

Figure 161: but alternatively can throw the attackers arm out of the way.

Figure 162: The defender then wraps her leg around the attackers head. She maintains control of the attackers head with her other hand.

Figure 163: The defender closes her guard to keep control of the attacker. She switches which hand has head control on the attacker. The defender now gets control of the attacker's free hand.

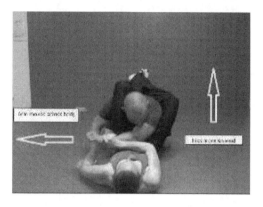

Figure 164: The defender pushes her hips skyward while maintaining control of the attacker. This creates space between herself and the attacker so that she can slide his free arm across her body and under his neck.

Figure 165: While maintaining position, the attacker pulls on the ankle of the leg that is looped around the back of the attacker's head. She pulls the ankle of this foot to a position behind the knee on the opposite leg. With practice, proper set-up, and flexibility you may be able to get the ankle in position without use of your hand. Set-up this way if needed.

Figure 166: The defender has put the leg in position. She looks the leg down.

Figure 167: This is the final position for the choke. The arm of the attacker acts as the choking device on one side while the defenders leg on the opposite side acts as the other choking device. These two devices cut off blood flow to the brain via the carotid arteries on either side of the neck. The defender pulls down on the head to apply more pressure to the choke. If the choke is not in proper position, do not stress. Adjust as needed. Just make sure to maintain control of the attacker. From this position, punches to the face of the attacker can be thrown as well.

Figure 168: Side view of positioning for the leg triangle choke.

Punch Block Defense

Figure 169: This is the start position for the punch defense in guard. The defender is holding the attacker in closed-guard with head control.

Figure 170: The attacker decides to attempt a punch. As the defender feels the attacker pull away for a punch, she instantly reaches for the attacking arm.

Figure 171: The defender takes hold of the attacker's hand. She holds the attacker's hand tight to her leg, effectively pinning the attacking arm in place with the knee.

Figure 172: The attacker decides to attempt a punch with the other hand and the defender pins this arm as well.

Figure 173: The defender now has control of both the attacker's arms. From here she could start to work for an arm bar or triangle choke. I will not go into that here but use your imagination and I am sure you can see the set-up.

Figure 174: The attacker decides to posture up (sit up). As he does, the defender keeps a hold of the hand and slides her knee between the attacker and herself.

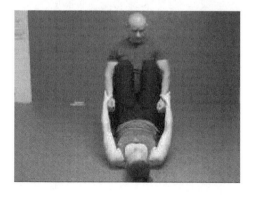

Figure 175: The attacker is now pinned between the defender's knees and hands. The defender could look for an attack here or she could let go.

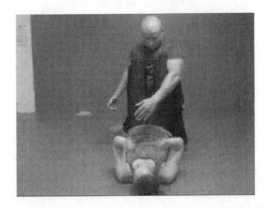

Figure 176: The defender releases the attacker's hands. The attacker does this since she knows the attacker cannot hit her as long as her legs are extended and he is on the other side. In this image, you can see that the attacker is too far away to reach the defenders face.

Figure 177: The attacker can reach the stomach but the amount of force that can be exerted in decreased. The defender can minimize this by further extending the knees by pushing the hips toward the sky more.

Figure 178: The attacker decides to go to his feet. The defender know this by the way the attacker's body shifts and the movement of his feet to a position from which he can begin to get up. The defender moves with him. She first pushes off with her knees, then as he stands up, she places her feet on his hips.

Figure 179: The attacker has stood up. The defender has her feet on his hips. Her legs are extended and she is actively keeping him at a distance using her leg strength. The legs need to be strong here. The legs should not be stiff but rather have a slight bend in the knee to move with attacker's body. The hands should be protecting the face. From this position, the attacker should not be able to hit the defender in the face.

Figure 180: The attacker attempts to punch the defender. Due to the defender keeping the attacker at a distance with her legs, the attacker is unable to reach the face of the defender or the stomach of the defender.

Figure 181: The defender may be able to slightly reach the stomach but, if the defender is keeping the attacker at a good distance, then the attacker will not be able to land blows that are solid.

Figure 182: As the attacker leans on the feet of the defender looking for strikes, the defender can time the punches and allow the attacker to fall into guard. The attacker will instantly put his hands out to catch himself. This only works if attacker is leaning on the feet. This is a surprise move that works by catching the attacker off-balance. If the attacker is not leaning on the feet, do not use this move. Instead, use the moves shown in the standing-in-guard section.

Figure 183: The defender has effectively pulled the attacker back into guard and can now work to sweep or attack.

A Quick Review

In this section you have learned:

1. What attacking from guard means.

2. How to defend punches from guard.

3. How to perform an arm bar from guard.

4. How to perform a triangle choke from guard.

Chapter 6: Attacks from mount

This next section will cover what to do once you have the attacker on their back. This will be essential to know once you have successfully swept an attacker who took you to the ground. Once you have completed on the sweeps on the attacker you will either be in mount, or in guard. What sweep you use, and what position you end up in on top, will determine your next move. There will be some similarities and some differences. As with the previous sections, I will refer to you as the defender and the other person as the attacker.

If you perform the elevator sweep, you will end up in the attacker's mount. From here, you can attack or attempt to get up. The best idea is to try to get up and get away from the situation. The quicker and further you can get away from the situation, and the attacker, the better chance of avoiding harm. However, it is not always possible to get away from an attacker. If you cannot get up to remove yourself from the situation, and you decide to stay in the mount position, you must know how to control the position. If you do not, the attacker could roll you over and end up back on top. Sweeping the attacker the second time around could prove more difficult. The next series of pictures will talk about positional control such as posting, swimming, etc.

Posting is the act of putting your limbs out to maintain balance and position. The following images will offer a brief introduction to this concept.

Figure 184: In this image, the defender has achieved mount. This likely occurred by using the elevator sweep. Now that she is on top, the defender wants to maintain the position. The attacker will try to reverse this position. In this image, the defender has her hand "posted" on the ground with her legs tight in mount position on the attacker's body.

Figure 185: In this image, the defender has lowered her center of gravity by "posting" her arms further out and lowering her body towards the attacker. This allows the defender to stay heavy on the attacker in order to prevent him pushing off to create space or from working for an attack.

Figure 186: Taking the previous image on step further, the defender has hooked her arm around the attacker's head. This creates a strong grip on the attacker that further strengthens the top position and will assist in keeping the attacker from creating space in an attempt to get away or work for an attack.

Figure 187: In this image, the attacker is attempting to roll the defender off him. As he rolls side to side, the defender moves with him, but only to stop the attacker from rolling her over. The defender posts her hand out to the side the attacker is attempting to roll. She pushes her knee in to the ground on the same side. This gives the defender two posts on the side that the attacker is trying to roll her. She hooks his opposite leg with her opposite leg so that he cannot scoot out the opposite side.

Figure 188: The attacker now rolls to the opposite side attempting to roll. The defender uses the same technique to defend the roll. Do this as many times as necessary until the attacker tires of trying or runs out of energy.

Low Swim

Figure 189: Once the attacker sees that he cannot roll the defender due to her posting ability he or she will look to free themselves in another way. Whether the attacker is skilled in jiu-jitsu or not, they may realize the need to trap the arm to get out of the bottom position.

Figure 190: The attacker attempts to trap the arm. The attacker may use a variety of techniques to do this.

Figure 191: The defender rotates her arm at the elbow. She brings the arm to the inside, which is away from the attacker's arm. She does Not bring her elbow toward the body. This gives the attacker the attempt to trap the arm next to the body.

Figure 192: The defender finishes the rotation and places the arm on the mat. Do this for either arm.

High Swim

Figure 193: The high swim is a defense to the attacker trying to push you off them in order to create space. The attacker may create space in an attempt to escape, to initiate an attack, or in an attempt to keep the defender from attacking.

Figure 194: The defender moves her left arm to the inside of the attacker's right arm. The goal here is to "snake" the arm to the inside and guide it toward the floor. She is not attempting to force the attackers arm by sheer muscle. Instead, she is guiding the attacker's arm out of the way by forcing her arm and shoulder through the space between the attacker's arm.

Figure 195: The defender has now placed the arm she snaked onto the floor. She is based out with this hand. The defender begins to "snake" her opposite arm through the attackers other arm.

Figure 196: The defender has now placed both hands in base on the ground. She is high in this position.

Figure 197: The defender came through high in the previous image. She alternatively can "snake" her arms through into a wider base and come in low. This gets the defender into a lower center of gravity to end in a heavier position on the attacker and stop the attacker from attempting to push off again.

Americana From Mount

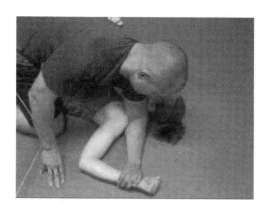

Figure 198: The Americana is another common submission in jiu-jitsu. Notice the placement of the elbow against the head of the attacker. The defender has a hold of the attacker's wrist.

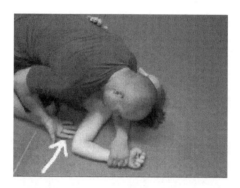

Figure 199: The defender reaches his hand under the attacker's arm.

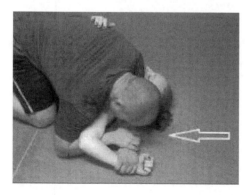

Figure 200: The defender grabs his wrist.

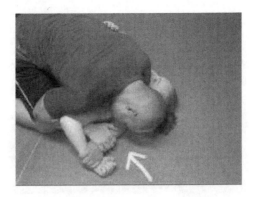

Figure 201: The defender now draws his hand back in a type of brushing motion in the direction of the arrow. As he does he lefts the attacker's arm and rotates the shoulder. This applies pressure to the elbow and shoulder. From this position, the defender can inflict serious damage on the attacker.

Strikes From The Mount

Figure 202: Once the defender has achieved a solid control of mount, she can look to attack the attacker. Punches from the mount are a successful attacking method. A straight punch to the face can stun or incapacitate an opponent.

Figure 203: In order to throw the punch the defender must posture up (sit up) in mount. From here, she can throw a straight punch.

Figure 204: Alternatively, she can throw a hook to the attacker's face. Elbows can also be thrown from the mount. If at any point that defender feels she is going to be rolled off by the attacker, she should lower her center and post back out to the start position.

Get Up From The Attacker's Guard

Figure 205: A defender who performs the trap and roll sweep will find themselves in the attacker's guard. From here the defender can perform a few techniques. One is the get up.

Figure 206: The get up from the attacker's mount is performed by first pushing off the attacker's chest.

Figure 207: The defender bring her knee between the attacker's leg and post her hand on the attacker's knee.

Figure 208: The attacker pushes off the attacker to hold him in place while getting her legs under her.

Figure 209: The defender stands up.

Although you should end up in guard or in the mount position once you have swept the attacker, you may find yourself in half guard. Attacks from half guard bear similarities to the attacks from mount. Personally, I would not recommend staying in half guard. I would recommend passing into side control or mount. However, you may find yourself in half-guard. Strikes can be thrown from half-guard and submissions can be attempted. A punch or elbow can be thrown. The Americana choke can be applied as well. To pass from this position you must pull the leg free from the attacker leg grip, the slide the knee upward and allow the leg to slide across the attackers belly and to the outside of their body. This will give you mount. There are more details for this position but, due to constraints for this manual, we will stop here for now.

A Quick Review:

In this section you have learned:

1. What attacking from mount means.

2. How to control top position.

3. How to do the low swim and high swim.

4. How to strike from mount.

5. How to do the Americana from mount.

6. How to get up from an opponent's guard.

Chapter 7: Putting it together

Now that you have learned the individual moves, it is time to put it all together. The following will suggest specific chains that are highly likely to occur in a street fight or competitive situation. For this section, I will not include more images. Refer back to the specific images for the moves listed in each sequence. I will walk you through some defensive and offensive sequences that you can perform.

While I write this manual with self-defense in mind, knowing how to attack is important. Some attackers will not stop unless you make them stop. I do not advocate violence in general, but there is a time for everything, including violence. If the time calls for it, use your best judgment and stop the person who wants to hurt you.

For defense:

1. If the attacker shoots in for a double leg takedown, use the head push and pivot to redirect the attacker's momentum and to move you out of their striking distance. From here, circle out and maintain the distance.

2. If the attacker shoots in for a double leg, succeeds in the takedown, and lands in your guard, then pull him or her into your closed guard and achieve head control. Perform the trap and roll sweep. From here, punch the attacker in the face and gut to hurt and stall him or her. Use the get up from the attacker's guard to get your feet. Step back to create distance between you and them.

3. If the attacker shoots in for a double leg, succeeds in the takedown, and lands in your guard, then pull him or her into your closed guard and achieve head control. Get control of one of the attacker's arms. Perform the arm bar from guard. Break the attacker's arm. Get up in base. Create distance between you and the attacker.

That is just a few examples of possible combos. With the moves that have been outlined in this manual there are many different possible combinations and variations that can be performed. Here are a few more quick examples for defense:

1. Attacker shoots double-defender is taken to ground-defender closes guard and achieves head control-defender attempts trap and roll unsuccessfully – defender performs triangle choke-opponent goes to sleep-defender gets up-defender creates space

2. Attacker achieves body clinch-defender creates space and punches-attacker pushes forward and achieves takedown-defender closes guard-attacker punches-defender uses punch block series-attacker is in standing position-defender uses leg hook takedown from guard-attacker is on ground-defender gets up in base-creates space

The list goes on. Be creative and see what combos work together. This will help you drill the moves in sequence as well as learn what move work best for you personally. What works for one person may not be the best for you and vice-versa. Experiment.

For attack:

For a moment, let us imagine that you performed any of the defensive sequences we just outlined. The attacker just will not stop. Apparently, he or she wants to get beat up. It looks like you are going to have to oblige. The following can work to help you do this.

1. Attacker is circling-defender punches attacker in the face a few times to stall and disorient him or her-defender performs the double leg takedown-defender moves into mount-defender punches attacker in face until he or she stop fighting back-defender performs the get up from mount

2. Attacker is circling-attacker attempts double leg-defender captures the attacker in the guillotine-defender chokes attacker until attacker stops fighting or passes out-defender uses snake arms then pushes attacker back if still awake-defender punches attacker in face until attacker goes down or stops fighting

These are just a couple of possible ways to make an attacker think twice about continuing to attack. In the end, you must defend yourself. Do what you have to do if necessary. Always exercise sound judgment. We do not want to fight unless a threat is present and cannot be avoided.

A Quick Review:

After reading this section you should:

1. Understand what chaining techniques means.

2. Know the importance of chaining techniques together.

3. Be using critical thinking to envision other chains of techniques.

4. Know how to use defensive chains.

5. Know how to do offensive chains.

6. Begin to understand how to continue when a technique fails.

Chapter 8: Cross training with standup attacks and defense

Every confrontation begins in a standing position. Many fights end up on the ground. You may not be able to prevent the fight from going to the ground. You may not be able to prevent it from staying standing. You should be prepared for both scenarios. If you are not able to stand and defend yourself, you may find yourself on the losing end of a beating. For this reason, it is necessary to know how to attack and defend from both positions.

The first thing a person should learn for stand up striking is how to stand in a standup striking exchange. For some it may seem a silly concept, that the way you stand makes a difference, but it is true nonetheless. A proper stance will result in an improved ability to move, strike, and defend. A proper stance will allow a person to move quicker and at better angles. A proper stance will result in greater power with strikes and will align the body to defend against strikes and takedowns. A proper stance will also allow a person to perform takedowns in a more explosive manner. The question then becomes what is the best stance. Now this depends on what method of fighting is being applied. A boxing stance is different from a wrestling stance, which is different from a Muay Thai stance.

The type of guard to be used will be an area of question as well. Standing the guard refers to the way a person holds their hands in accordance to their face for the purpose of defending and attacking. The three basic guards are low guard, medium guard, and high guard. Multiple variations of each guard, as well as other hand positioning, may be used. For example, a wrestler or grappler will traditionally use a hand positioning where the arms are outreached. This allows the person to grab their opponent for a takedown or other attack. This is not the best way to defend against strikes, however.

For the purposes of this manual, an MMA stance with a high guard will be used. An MMA stance is meant to be an equally efficient stance for multiple purposes including striking, takedown defense, and takedowns. The next series of photos will outline the proper stance and guard for both the orthodox and southpaw stances. The orthodox position is the standard position for a right-handed person. In it, the right leg and hand are kept back with the left hand and foot kept forward. The southpaw is the exact opposite position and is meant for a left-handed person. The following images will outline the stances and related guard.

Figure 210: This is a basic MMA stance. The legs are spread in a wider than shoulder width stance, the knees are slightly bent, hands are held in high guard, and the chin is tucked.

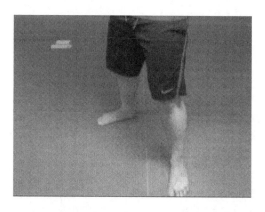

Figure 211: This is the foot position for the basic MMA stance for an orthodox (right-hand) person. I have aligned myself with the tapeline in the mat so that you can have a better perception of how the feet line-up. The front foot and rear foot are on opposite sides of the line. The front foot is pointed in a forward direction. The rear foot is angled outward from the body in a slightly forward direction. You can clearly see that the front knee has a slight bend in it, although this is hard to see with the rear knee.

Figure 212: The basic MMA stance again. This time from a Southpaw (left-handed) person. The only thing that changes is which foot/hand is forward and which foot/hand is back.

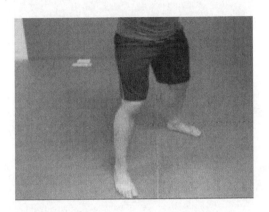

Figure 213: The footing for the basic MMA stance again. This time from a Southpaw (left-handed) person. The only thing that changes are which foot is forward and which foot is back.

Defense is the second part of standup and arguably the most important. It does not matter that you can attack if you do not know how to defend. Defense will protect you from harm and allow you to set up strikes. The next series of photos will show some common defense and avoidance techniques used in stand up striking such as the rock back, hook block, and others.

Slipping

Figure 214: Here I am in the high guard start position. We will start with illustrating the slip. The slip is a common boxing defense maneuver used to evade straight punches, which are the jab and cross.

Figure 215: The slip involves moving slightly to the side to avoid a shot that comes straight down the middle toward your face. The slip will move you just enough to one side or the other to avoid the punch.

Figure 216: There is no need for a huge bend or dip to the side. This is unnecessary and wastes reaction time. Always slip to the outside of the punch as well. If you slip to the inside of a punch, you could slip right into a second punch.

Figure 217: Return to start position.

The Bob-N-Weave

Figure 218: The bob-n-weave is another staple in boxing defense. In requires a person to move their head and upper body in a half-circle downward motion. This is used to avoid a hook thrown toward the head. When timed properly the bob-n-weave will result in the hook moving above the head without causing any damage.

Figure 219: In this image, I am circling to my left. This would be used to avoid a punch coming from my right side.

Figure 220: I continue circling. I am at mid-point. Ideally, the punch would be overhead right now. I am moving to my right.

Figure 221: I am coming up on my right. The punch would be off to my left at this point and I would have completely avoided it.

Figure 222: Return to start position.

The Rock-Back

Figure 223: The next defensive maneuver is the rock-back. It is a simple move that can be used to avoid any type of punch when timed properly.

Figure 224: For this move the user simply leans back to avoid whatever punch is thrown.

Figure 225: Return to start position.

The Jab

Figure 226: The first strike to be covered will be the jab. This is the start position for the jab and all other punches.

Figure 227: The jab is simple in principle but will require practice to perfect speed, power, and timing. When throwing the jab the front hand is extended straight out from the body as shown in the image. The head is kept tucked low. The non-punching hand is kept tight to the face for protection. The jab can be thrown standing still, with a forward lean, or when moving.

Figure 228: This is a view of the jab from the outside. Notice how the shoulder of the jabbing arm is kept high and tight to the face. This protects the face from attack while the arm is extended. Even when attacking, defense is important. To some people, defense is more important when attacking, since attacks generally leave a person open to a counter attack.

Figure 229: Return the jabbing hand to start position in a straight line. Do not drop the hand. Do not leave the hand in the extended position. As fast as the hand is extended for the punch is as fast as it should return to the start position.

The Cross

Figure 230: The dynamics of the cross are essentially the same as the jab, just with the opposite hand.

Figure 231: The punch comes straight out. Notice the shoulder is high and protects the face.

Figure 232: The opposite side view of the cross when extended. Notice how the hand is high and protecting the face.

Figure 233: Return to the start position.

A Quick Review:

In this section you have learned:

1. The importance of cross training.

2. What stand up striking is.

3. What a proper stance is.

4. How to evade striking attacks.

5. How to perform basic punches.

Conclusion

That is it. A brief introduction to jiu-jitsu has been given to you with a little bit of stand-up for diversity. Keep in mind that this is just a small part of what is available. As you learn, take pride in that learning but do not let it go to your head. The point of this manual is not to teach you to be a douchebag who wants to beat somebody up. The goal is to teach you to defend yourself against the douchebag. Train hard and train safe.

Author the Expert

Nathan DeMetz is a 32-year-old fitness enthusiast and martial arts practitioner from Indiana. He has been weight lifting for 10 years and practicing martial arts for almost 3. In 2010, Nathan started his martial arts journey with private boxing lessons from a local instructor before moving on to Muay Thai and jiu-jitsu. He is a white belt in jiu-jitsu and has near 3 years of combined kickboxing experience. Nathan always looks to improve his skills through research, one-on-one conversation, and practical application. Nathan competed in small-scale local competitions though he is not a competitive athlete in general. He simply enjoys the thrill of learning and practicing new forms of martial arts as well as the rush he gets from weight lifting. Personal bests in weight training include a 500 lb squat, 345 lb bench, and a 530 deadlift at a bodyweight between 185 lbs to 213 lbs.

Outside of athletics, Nathan is a family man and everyday guy. He has a 2-year Business degree that he has used in management and now as a self-employed contractor. He primarily provides Internet based services to online clients. His list of clients includes Google, Ask.com and eBay. He is married and has been with his wife, Grace, for almost 7 years. Nathan has a daughter from a previous relationship who will be fifteen by the time this manual goes to publication. Also by the time of publication Nathan will be a Certified Personal Trainer (CPT) with the International Sports Sciences Association (ISSA). Nathan had the opportunity to meet and learn from a USAPL state ranked power lifter, two NPC bodybuilding competitors, and other local, amateur, and competitive athletes.

Away from work and training, Nathan enjoys spending time with his wife and daughter. He enjoys fat burgers with French fires and juicy steaks.

HowExpert publishes quick 'how to' guides on all topics from A to Z by everyday experts. Visit HowExpert.com to learn more.

Recommended Resources

- HowExpert.com – Quick 'How To' Guides on All Topics from A to Z by Everyday Experts.
- HowExpert.com/free – Free HowExpert Email Newsletter.
- HowExpert.com/books – HowExpert Books
- HowExpert.com/courses – HowExpert Courses
- HowExpert.com/clothing – HowExpert Clothing
- HowExpert.com/membership – HowExpert Membership Site
- HowExpert.com/affiliates – HowExpert Affiliate Program
- HowExpert.com/writers – Write About Your #1 Passion/Knowledge/Expertise & Become a HowExpert Author.
- HowExpert.com/resources – Additional HowExpert Recommended Resources
- YouTube.com/HowExpert – Subscribe to HowExpert YouTube.
- Instagram.com/HowExpert – Follow HowExpert on Instagram.
- Facebook.com/HowExpert – Follow HowExpert on Facebook.

Made in the USA
Columbia, SC
27 January 2025

52714326R00074